About the Book

It's hard to believe that it was less than three decades ago when a chimpanzee was put into suborbital flight. And this was to pave the way for Astronaut John Glenn, who on February 20, 1962, was the first man placed in orbit. Just seven years later, man walked on the moon.

With Space Shuttles *Columbia* and *Challenger* making regular flights, Voyager 2 expected to arrive at the planet Neptune as soon as 1989 and satellites now bringing us television and the weather, it is apparent that outer space is increasingly a part of all our daily lives.

In spectacular NASA photographs and a probing and comprehensive text, Melvin Berger looks at the incredible technology and advancements of the space program, and brings us closer to the fascinating exploration, discoveries and mysteries of just what's "out there" in our miraculous universe.

MELVIN BERGER

Space Shots, Shuttles and Satellites

G. P. PUTNAM'S SONS   NEW YORK

For everyone at NASA
who is working to make
the dream of space a reality.

PHOTO CREDITS

*The author wishes to express his sincere appreciation to NASA
for the cover photograph and the photographs appearing in the book,
with the exception of the photographs on pages 67 and 69,
which were furnished by NOAA (National Oceanic and Atmospheric Administration)*

Copyright © 1983 by Melvin Berger
All rights reserved. Published simultaneously in
Canada by General Publishing Co. Limited, Toronto.
Printed in the United States of America
Second Impression
Book design by Mike Suh

Library of Congress Cataloging in Publication Data
Berger, Melvin.
Space shots, shuttles and satellites.
Includes index.
Summary: Discusses the first quarter-century of our
space program, what is happening now, and what is planned
for the future.
1. Astronautics—United States—Juvenile literature.
[1. Astronautics] I. Title.
TL789.8.U5B45   1983   629.4'09   83-19279
ISBN 0-399-61210-6

CONTENTS

INTRODUCTION 6

■ *SPACE SHOTS* ■

1. BECOMING AN ASTRONAUT 9
2. ROCKET FIRE 14
3. BREAKING FREE 17
4. SKYLAB AND BEYOND 25

■ *SHUTTLES* ■

5. COUNTDOWN 31
6. THE SPACE SHUTTLE 39
7. SHUTTLES AT WORK 45

■ *SATELLITES* ■

8. INTRODUCTION TO SATELLITES 53
9. COMMUNICATION SATELLITES 56
10. SCIENTIFIC, WEATHER AND MILITARY SATELLITES 62

GLOSSARY 74

INDEX 78

Fremont Public Library
FREMONT, MICH.

INTRODUCTION

The title of this book is a tongue twister. Try saying it three times fast—space shots, shuttles and satellites, space shots, shuttles and satellites, space shots, shuttles and satellites—and see how mixed up you get.

Why write a book with a tongue twister title?

Because it sums up perfectly one of the greatest scientific achievements of all time—the conquest of outer space.

Humans first reached into space with a number of space shots. The initial attempt was the launch of Sputnik 1 by the Soviet Union in October 1957. The next year President Dwight D. Eisenhower set up NASA (National Aeronautics and Space Administration) to develop an American space program.

In quick succession, NASA launched a number of highly successful unmanned exploratory space shots: Explorer (starting January 1958), Pioneer (starting October 1958), Mariner (starting August 1962), Viking (starting August 1975) and Voyager (starting August 1977).

Among NASA's most spectacular space shots were three series of manned spaceflights: Mercury (May 1961 to May 1963), Gemini (March 1965 to November 1966) and Apollo (October 1968 to December 1972), which climaxed with the manned landing on the moon in July 1969.

The first orbital test of the Space Shuttle was held in April 1981. The

Shuttle is designed to carry objects and people into space and to return them to earth. One special advantage of the Space Shuttle is that it can be used over and over. Since November 1982, Space Shuttles have been launched according to a regular schedule. As soon as each one accomplishes its mission and returns to earth, it is made ready for its next launch.

Satellites—objects that enter into orbit around the earth—have been part of the space program from the beginning. But in the 1980s they were recognized as a vital communication link throughout the world. Today they carry TV and radio signals, telephone conversations and printed words and pictures; they make weather observations, conduct scientific research and serve military functions.

It has taken just over a quarter of a century to progress from our first steps into space to our conquest of the vast region beyond our planet earth. How we got there, what we are doing in space, and what is planned for the future is the story of this book.

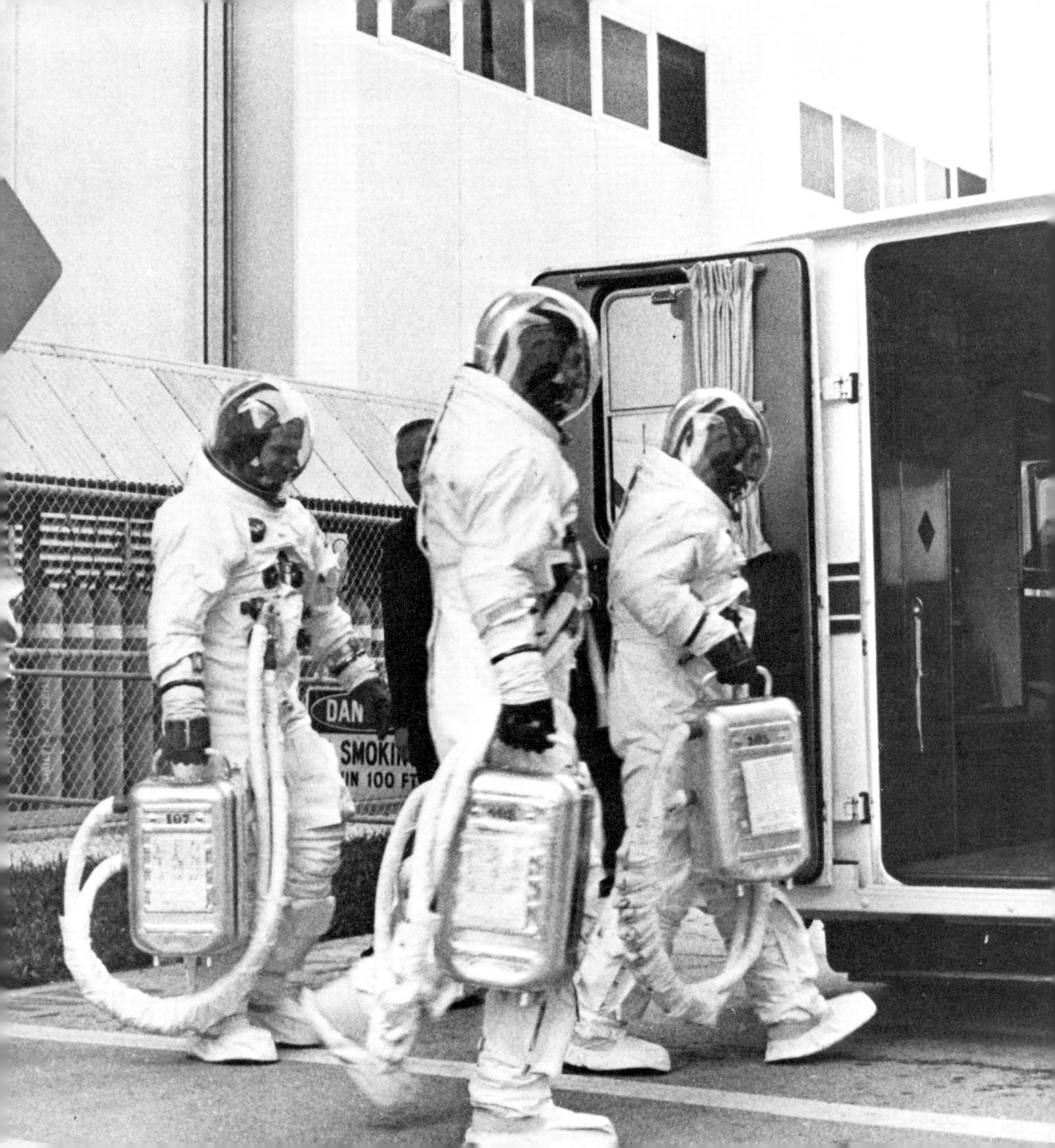

SPACE SHOTS

1
BECOMING AN ASTRONAUT

Are you under thirty-five? Are you between five feet and six feet four inches tall? Are you in top physical condition? Do you have a college degree in engineering, science or math? Can you pass psychological tests that show you are in good mental health?

If so, you can apply to become an astronaut in America's space program.

Have you flown a jet aircraft for at least 1,000 hours? Then you may qualify as a pilot astronaut. Pilot astronauts handle the controls of the orbiter in space shuttle missions.

Do you hold an advanced college degree in science, or have you had three years' experience in scientific research? Perhaps you will become a mission or payload specialist. You will carry out the various mission operations and scientific experimental tasks on shuttle flights.

For the latest information on becoming an astronaut—either a pilot or mission specialist—you can write to:

Astronaut Candidate Program
Code AHX
NASA Johnson Space Center
Houston, TX 77058

Once you are selected as a pilot or as a mission or payload specialist candidate, you have to go back to school. Most of your training, which may last two years or more, takes place at the Lyndon B. Johnson Space Center in Houston, Texas. It is operated by NASA (National Aeronautics and Space Administration), the agency of the United States government that controls all our nation's civilian space activities. (The U.S. Air Force has a Space Command that oversees the military applications of space.)

At the Johnson Space Center you are given advanced courses in such subjects as mathematics, meteorology or weather science, astronomy, physics, computer science and navigation.

You are also taught how to get along in a state of weightlessness, or zero-gravity. You will be weightless most of your time in space, and that takes some getting used to. The funny feeling that you get in your stomach when you are in a high-speed elevator going down very fast or in a roller coaster starting its descent after a steep climb is something like the sensation of being weightless.

As an astronaut in training you are taken for plane rides in which the plane flies up and then down through a parabolic curve. As the plane goes "over the top" of the curve, you float in the cabin and experience the feeling of zero-gravity for up to thirty seconds.

During these brief periods, you practice handling the various pieces of equipment you will use on your mission. You also learn how to move about in zero-gravity by pulling or pushing your way around. Another part of this training is to relearn, under conditions of zero-gravity, such simple actions as dressing, washing, eating and drinking. Without gravity keeping the objects in place, each of these tasks becomes very difficult.

Some of your zero-gravity training is done in a huge indoor water tank. Here you wear a special space suit that is similar to an old diving suit. Because of the buoyancy of the water, you float in the tank just as you would float in the spacecraft in outer space. You find out how to accomplish the various mission tasks, from piloting the craft to preparing meals, in this special environment.

Part of your training is to become familiar with every part of the construction of the spacecraft, the launch vehicle and the payload your mission will be carrying. You attend engineering conferences at the Johnson Space Center. You visit the offices and factories of the scientists and manufacturers who are preparing the equipment for future space shots. Like all the other candidates, you concentrate on just one aspect of the program, and become an "expert" on that subject. Then you take your turn reporting the findings to the others. Eventually everyone has some knowledge of each phase of the coming flight.

Although the entire space program is geared to running successful missions, you are also prepared to handle all possible problems—for example, you are taught about water survival. Should a mission abort right after launch or should the returning spacecraft crash land in the ocean, you must be able to stay afloat until help arrives.

After a few months of training, you may be picked to be part of a crew for a particular flight. Now you are taught that flying in space is like parachute jumping. You must do it absolutely right the very first time. There is no second chance.

(left) Part of an astronaut's training is to learn how to get along in a state of weightlessness or zero-gravity.

(right) Astronauts are taught how to survive in the water in case of an accident.

In addition to mastering every single task in the mission, you also receive "cross-training." Each person in the crew has to be prepared to handle the duties of the others, should anybody run into trouble. Meanwhile, a second crew is receiving exactly the same training as your crew. Should one person or the entire first crew not go on the mission, the second, or backup, crew is ready to step in without delay.

During the final stretch of training, you spend many hours in a replica of the spacecraft cabin, called a simulator. The simulator has the same controls and dials and buttons as the spacecraft and through its windows you see space precisely as it looks hundreds of miles from earth. In the simulator you go through each step you will follow while in space, except that you remain firmly anchored to the ground in the Space Center at Houston.

The various instruments in the simulator and the views you see through the windows are controlled by a computer. The computer is programmed to give you the readings and the views you would get during an actual mission. If you operate the simulator correctly, everything will appear to go well. But, should you throw the wrong switch, problems may occur, and it's up to you to set things right. The training in the simulator is so thorough that it will make the actual mission seem second nature—almost!

A few weeks before the date of blast-off, the simulator is hooked up to NASA's Mission Control Center. This is the computer installation that is connected to the worldwide network of tracking stations that will guide the actual flight. Now the entire NASA team goes through the whole mission from blast-off to landing, as a final rehearsal of the actual flight.

Finally, it is the big day, the day of your space shot. You get your last-minute instructions, don your space suit, and follow the countdown until it's time for you to enter the spacecraft.

Soon you are inside. Until launch time you keep very busy checking every system and piece of equipment. You check and recheck that everything is in perfect working order.

Then comes the most thrilling moment of all—T–Zero. The rocket beneath you roars to life. A ferocious red-orange flame leaps out and spreads

over the ground. Your spacecraft quivers and vibrates. Then, ever so slowly, it begins to rise off the pad.

Gradually it picks up speed. The acceleration pins you tightly against your curved seat. In a few minutes, you are soaring, far above the rapidly shrinking earth beneath you. You are embarked on the greatest adventure—a flight into the mystery and drama of outer space.

2
ROCKET FIRE

For most of the millions of years humans have lived on this planet, we have been firmly rooted to the earth. Then, in the late eighteenth century, balloons carried humans up into the sky. But it wasn't until the early years of this century, with the invention of the airplane, that we were truly able to break free.

As aviation advanced, airplanes were able to fly higher and higher. Although some advanced planes can reach altitudes of over 23 miles (37 km), and perhaps even higher, there is a limit to the height they can reach. No plane that is powered by jet engines or propellers will ever be able to fly beyond the upper limits of the earth's atmosphere.

The atmosphere is the envelope of air that completely surrounds the earth. The higher you go in the atmosphere, the thinner the air. Above about 200 or 300 miles (322 or 483 km) the air is too thin to support flight. Jet engines do not have the oxygen they need to burn the fuel and push their planes forward. And the air is too thin to offer the resistance the propeller blades need for flight.

Outer space is said to begin above the earth's atmosphere. Airplanes cannot fly there. The only way to reach that height is by means of a rocket.

The rockets used in space shots are very much like jet engines, with one major difference: Space rockets carry their own oxygen supply, or oxidizer. They don't depend on the oxygen in the air.

The Redstone booster rocket was used to launch the early American space shots.

Rockets—and jets, too—work according to a law of nature that was first stated by Sir Isaac Newton (1642–1727): For every action, there is an equal and opposite reaction. Suppose you stand on very slippery ice and throw a heavy rock forward. The action will cause a reaction that sends you sliding backwards on the ice.

Closer to illustrating the principle of the rocket engine is a simple experiment you can try. Blow up a balloon. Hold the balloon with your fingers pinching the neck closed. Now let go. What happens? The balloon flies madly about. The reason is that the compressed air that was inside the balloon escapes. As the air rushes out of the balloon, the equal and opposite reaction is for the balloon itself to fly forward. Without any guidance system, though, it spins around in all directions.

In the rocket a fuel, either liquid or solid, is burned in a hollow chamber. The combustion produces a large volume of hot gases. The gases expand or grow bigger. They force their way out through a narrow nozzle in the back of the rocket engine. The equal and opposite reaction shoves the rocket forward.

The idea of rockets dates back nearly 800 years to the ancient Chinese. Many of the early fireworks were really solid-fuel rockets. But the development of rockets in modern times that led directly to space shots came in the early decades of the twentieth century. A Russian high-school teacher, Konstantin E. Tsiolkovsky (1857–1935), developed the theory of rocket flight. The American physicist Robert H. Goddard (1882–1945) later carried out many experiments that established the practical, scientific basis for all future space flight.

During World War II scientists in several countries, including the United States, Germany and Russia, were developing rockets. They used them, rather than planes, to deliver high explosives to distant targets. The improvements in rocket design and construction through these years made possible the first true space flights.

3
BREAKING FREE

The advances in rocket technology that came as a result of World War II set the stage for the first human effort to explore outer space—Sputnik 1. Sputnik was a small, 184-pound (83.5-kg) metal sphere that was launched by the Russians on October 4, 1957, into a circular orbit around the earth. Its battery-operated radio transmitter sent out sad-sounding beeps that were heard on radio receivers around the world. Sputnik orbited at a height of nearly 600 miles (965 km) and moved at a speed of about 18,000 miles an hour (29,000 km). After twenty-three days the batteries failed. Sputnik orbited in silence for another seventy days, then fell to earth, burning up on reentry.

On November 3, 1957, less than a month after their first success, the Soviets launched Sputnik 2. This major triumph placed a living creature, a dog named Laika, into space. The Russian scientists discovered that life can safely exist in space, even though Laika died after about one week, probably due to a lack of oxygen. Three and one-half years later, on April 12, 1961, Russia once again stunned the world when twenty-seven-year-old army pilot Yuri Gagarin became the first human in space. Gagarin flew a 108-minute orbit around earth in the spaceship Vostok.

The United States had nothing to compare to the Russians' effort. The first attempt by American scientists, on December 6, 1957, to lift an unmanned

Still in his capsule, Ham is being removed from the spacecraft after the Mercury 2 flight.

rocket was a dismal failure. The spaceship exploded after barely rising off the launch pad.

On January 31, 1958, Americans enjoyed their first success with the unmanned Explorer 1 space shot. Eager to close the gap with Russia, the United States undertook a program to place a person in space. It was named the Mercury Project.

The first Mercury mission was unmanned. On the second, the chimpanzee Ham was sent up and safely recovered. This paved the way for the first manned space attempt.

The date was May 5, 1961, and the goal was modest. Astronaut Alan B. Shepard, Jr., was to be sent up to a height of only 115 miles (185 km), for a fifteen-minute suborbital flight. The ascent and return were completely satisfactory.

After one more suborbital attempt, the Mercury Project directors decided to undertake the most difficult test of all—placing a man in orbit. On the fateful day, February 20, 1962, Astronaut John H. Glenn hurtled into space in the tiny Mercury capsule. In a flight that lasted nearly five hours, Glenn completed three orbits around earth. Nearly five years of very hard work had brought the United States to the same place in space exploration as the Russians.

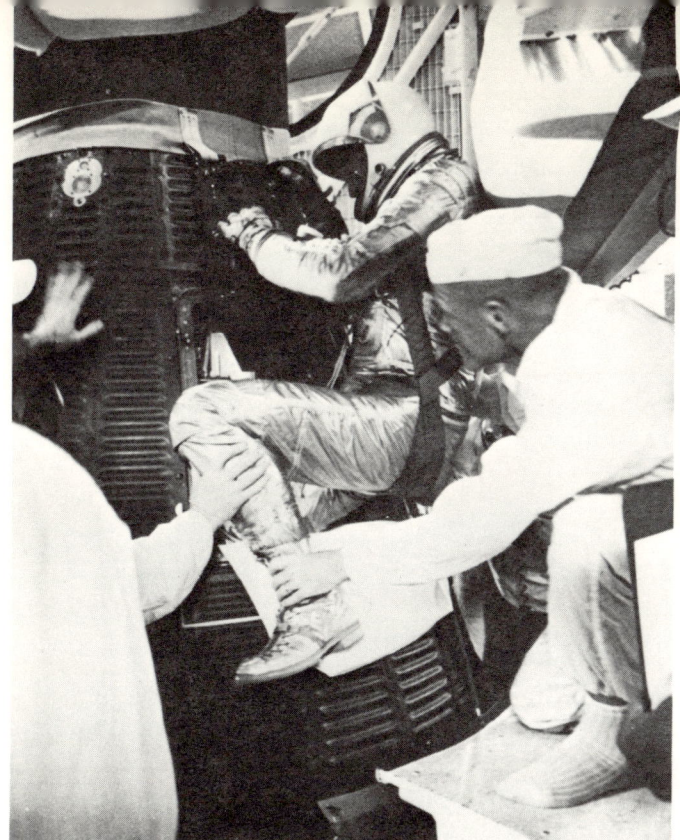 

Three more Mercury missions took place after Glenn's historic effort. The first one, Mercury 7, on May 24, 1962, lasted three orbits, too. For Mercury 8, on October 3, 1962, Astronaut Walter M. Schirra, Jr., finished six orbits in nine hours before landing only 4.5 miles (7 km) from the target. Mercury 9 extended from May 15 to 16, 1963. The object was to learn whether a human could spend a full day in space. Astronaut L. Gordon Cooper, Jr., completed 21 orbits in 34 hours, 20 minutes, proving that it was indeed possible.

By now the United States was beginning to pull ahead of the Soviet Union. President John F. Kennedy announced that America had set itself the target of having a man on the moon before 1970. A series of space shots, Project Apollo, was planned to achieve this long-range goal. But first a number of smaller steps were necessary. The Gemini series of twelve space shots, starting in 1964, was designed to pave the way for Project Apollo.

(left) Astronaut Alan B. Shepard, Jr. squeezes into the tiny Mercury capsule for NASA's first manned space flight.

(right) On February 20, 1962, Astronaut John H. Glenn became the first man in orbit.

Gemini 4 flight crew members McDivitt and White have their spacesuits checked before the flight.

Project Gemini began with two test firings. Then, on March 23, 1965, a two-man crew in an expanded Mercury capsule flew Gemini 3 in a three-orbit flight. To demonstrate the advanced controls, the astronauts changed course in midflight. Gemini 4, which lasted from June 3 to 7, 1965, was a milestone. Not only did it show that people could live in space for four days, but Astronaut Edward H. White's twenty-minute walk in space pointed to the possibility of working outside the vehicle while in orbit. The next mission, Gemini 5, lasted nearly eight days, from August 21 to 29, 1965. The craft made 120 orbits, and for the first time used fuel cells to get electric power.

Before the launch of Gemini 6, an unmanned rocket, Agena, was to be placed in orbit. Then the crew of Gemini 6 was to meet, or rendezvous, with Agena. Unfortunately, Agena failed to get into orbit, and splashed down into the Atlantic Ocean instead.

What happened next in Project Gemini shows how space scientists have to be ready to change their plans and make fast decisions when things don't work out as planned. The mission directors quickly decided to remove Gemini 6 from the launch pad, and send up Gemini 7 with its normal crew of two in place of Agena. Eleven days later, Gemini 6A, as Gemini 6 was now called, completed a successful rendezvous with Gemini 7. Astronaut Walter M. Schirra, Jr., on Gemini 6A maneuvered to within 0.39 inches (1 cm) of the other craft.

Gemini 8 advanced the space program one more notch. The space capsule actually docked, or attached itself to another Agena that had been placed in orbit. With that, the remaining Gemini shots, numbers 9 through 12, were able to develop further the maneuvers necessary for rendezvous and docking.

The greatest altitude ever reached by a Gemini space shot was 739 miles (1,190 km). Although this was quite remarkable, it fell far short of reaching the moon, which is 230,000 (370,000 km) from earth. To span this vast distance, NASA now undertook Project Apollo.

A spectacular walk in space by Astronaut Edward H. White II during the 1965 flight of Gemini 4.

Project Apollo got off to a calamitous start. During a prelaunch test on January 27, 1967, there was an explosion in the capsule. The three astronauts inside, Roger B. Chaffee, Virgil I. Grissom and Edward H. White II, were killed instantly. Ironically, this tragic loss of life, the first in America's space program, occurred on the ground.

Of course, the disaster set back the project for some time. It was not until October 1968 that the first manned Apollo flight was ready to lift off its launch pad for an eleven-day mission of 163 orbits.

The next flight, Apollo 8, departed on December 21, 1968, the first one destined for the moon. The ship was powered by the Saturn, an awesome rocket 363 feet (111 m) long, with the Apollo spacecraft. The rocket had three separate stages. The first stage developed the incredible thrust of 7.5 million pounds (33.3 million newtons) to get the Apollo off the pad. After two and one half minutes, the second stage took over, with one million pounds (4.5 million newtons) of thrust. Six minutes later the final stage kicked on, producing 200,000 pounds (890,000 newtons) of thrust. The Apollo 8 made ten orbits around the moon before coming back.

It remained for the two following Apollo missions, numbers 9 and 10, to check out the dependability of the lunar module. This miniature spaceship was to leave the main craft, called the command module, and land on the moon. Meanwhile, the command module continued in moon orbit. When the stay on the moon was over, the lunar module was to blast off its surface and dock with the command module. The two modules would then make the return journey to earth.

With all the preparatory work successfully completed, the project was ready for Apollo 11, the climax of the entire series. On July 20, 1969, the lunar module made a perfect soft landing on the moon. Astronaut Neil Armstrong became the first human being to set foot on the moon. His famous words, "That's one small step for a man, one giant leap for mankind," convey the universal pride in this historic feat.

Over the succeeding three and one-half years a total of twelve astronauts walked on the moon in five more Apollo landings. Each one was at a different site and for a longer period of time. The astronauts left various scientific measuring instruments on the lunar surface to send back data useful to scientists on earth. Also, the astronauts brought back samples of moon soil and rocks to be analyzed in earth laboratories.

Many feared that either the men or the samples would introduce deadly foreign germs to earth. Therefore, much care was taken to isolate both the men and the materials until the NASA scientists were certain that no moon bugs had taken the ride down to earth. After it was found that no living microbes were present, the astronauts were allowed to join their families and the soil and rock samples were released for study.

Neil Armstrong sets up measuring instruments on the moon surface after the amazing lunar landing on July 20, 1969. The lunar module is in the background.

(right) The Apollo capsule marks its return from the moon with a splashdown in the Atlantic Ocean.

(below) Astronaut Edwin E. Aldrin, Jr. talks to his family from the isolation unit.

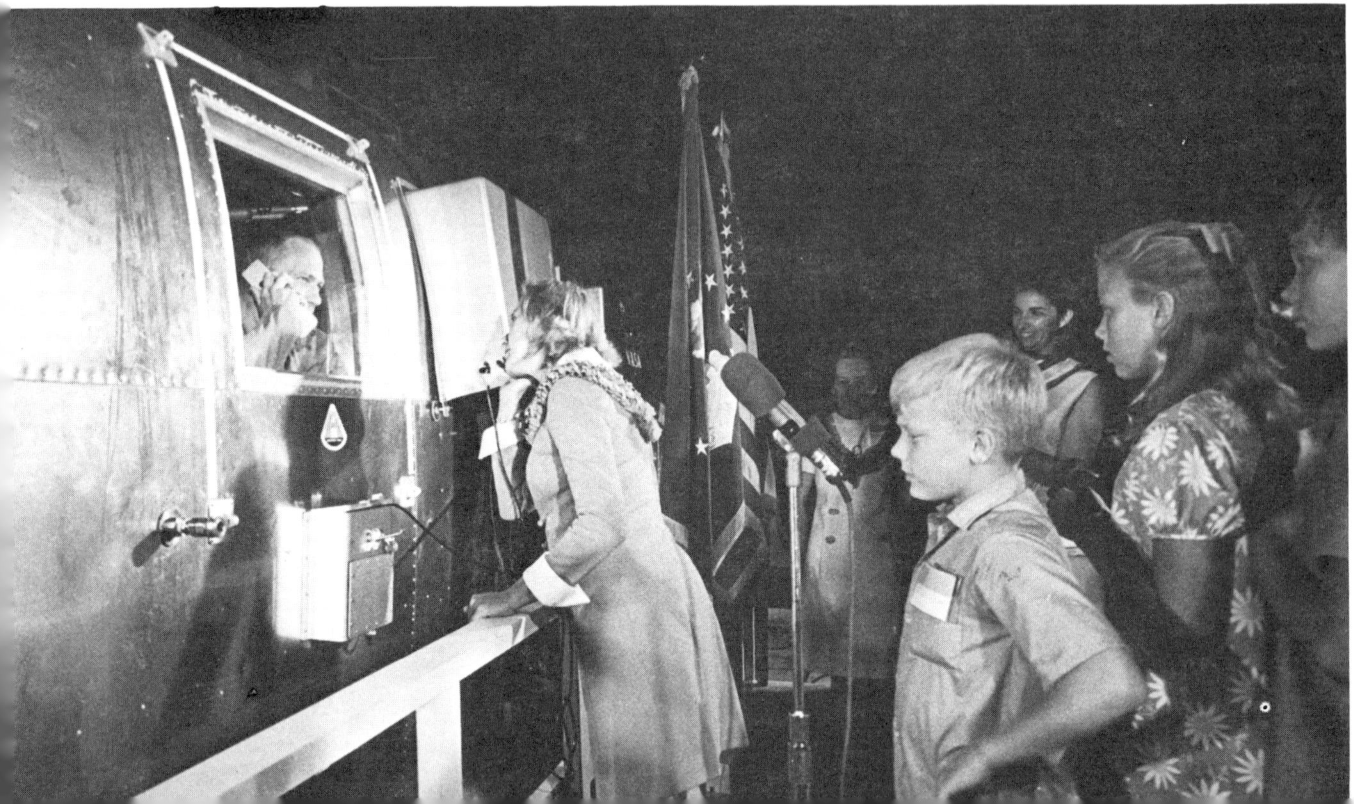

4
SKYLAB AND BEYOND

The Apollo landings on the moon before the deadline year 1970 fulfilled the national goal set by President Kennedy. But there were still many questions that space scientists wanted answered: How long can a human safely remain in space? What are the physical and psychological risks of space travel? What tasks are possible in the space environment? And what scientific information can be collected from a position in space?

To obtain the replies, NASA planned a series of four Skylab space shots for 1973 and 1974. An unmanned laboratory (48 feet [15 m] long and 22 feet [7 m] across) was placed in orbit on May 14, 1973. Inside were both living quarters for a three-member crew and a workshop for scientific experiments. Skylab was placed in an orbit 270 miles (434 km) above earth. The next day, three astronauts were to be rocketed up. The plan was to dock with the orbiting workshop, and to spend a period of time living there and doing various experiments.

Unfortunately, the force and heat of the blast-off badly damaged the workshop. There was some question whether it was in good enough condition to receive and hold the astronauts. For ten days the experts delayed the flight while they studied the radio signals that were coming back from the crippled craft. What was the exact nature and extent of the damage? Could it be repaired? Would the astronauts be safe in the damaged

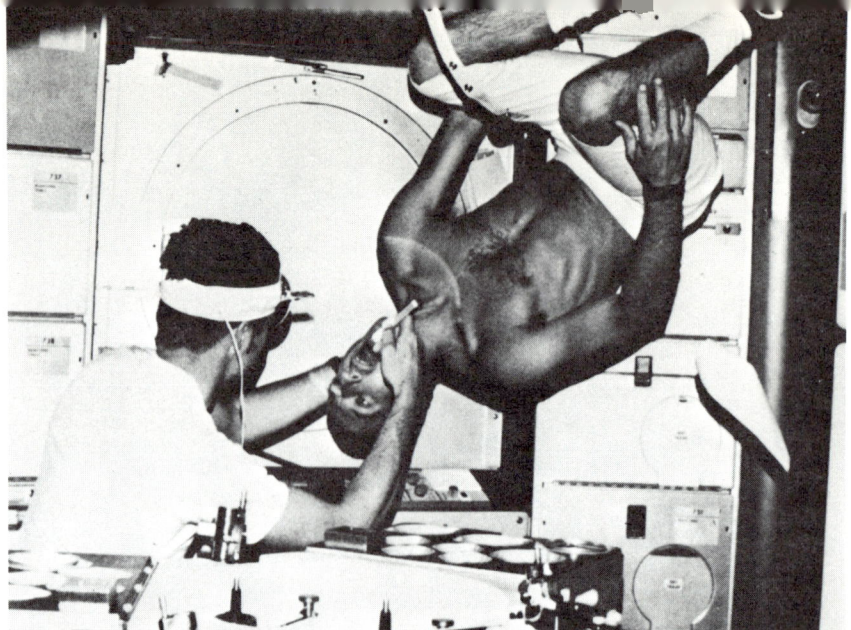

In the zero-gravity of Skylab, Astronaut Joseph P. Kerwin, M.D., examines Astronaut Charles Conrad, Jr., who is floating upside down in the cabin.

workshop? Finally, they decided to go for launch. The first Skylab crew was rocketed into space on May 25.

After first carrying out the necessary repairs with the greatest skill and courage, the three men—Charles C. Conrad, Jr., Joseph P. Kerwin and Paul J. Weitz—spent nearly a month in the world's first orbiting space station. Other crews followed on July 28 and November 16. The last one stayed in orbit for a record-breaking eighty-four days.

The Skylab series proved beyond any doubt that humans could spend long periods of time in space without danger. The astronauts did not show any ill effects from the zero-gravity. In fact, they collected much valuable data on what happens to the body over long periods of weightlessness. Further, without the interference of the earth's atmosphere, they were able to make many new astronomical observations. From their lofty position, they put together planetwide surveys of the earth's resources. Among other things, they learned that an industrial process such as the manufacture of absolutely round ball bearings was more easily possible in the zero-gravity of space than on earth, where gravity pulls the ball bearings slightly out of shape.

The completion of the Skylab missions brought to a triumphant conclusion the first stage in the manned space program.

Unmanned Space Shots

Everyone who reads science fiction knows about strange creatures from Mars who land on earth from time to time. While space scientists do not fear an attack from Mars, they certainly want to learn more about the planet, our nearest neighbor in space. What's more, they hope that their findings will tell them more about planet earth.

NASA launched two unmanned Viking space shots in late summer 1975 to probe the planet Mars. In addition to the booster rockets, each Viking consisted of an orbiter, designed to go into orbit around Mars, and a lander, built to land on the planet's surface and remain there forever.

The landers came down about 3,100 miles (5,000 km) apart. For one year they served as completely automatic, self-contained laboratories. The scientific equipment measured the weather on Mars—wind direction and velocity, pressure, temperature and humidity. Various instruments tracked marsquakes, which are like earthquakes, but on the red planet. A robot arm that extended out from the lander scooped up soil and rock samples. The cameras on board the Viking craft took thousands of pictures of surface features.

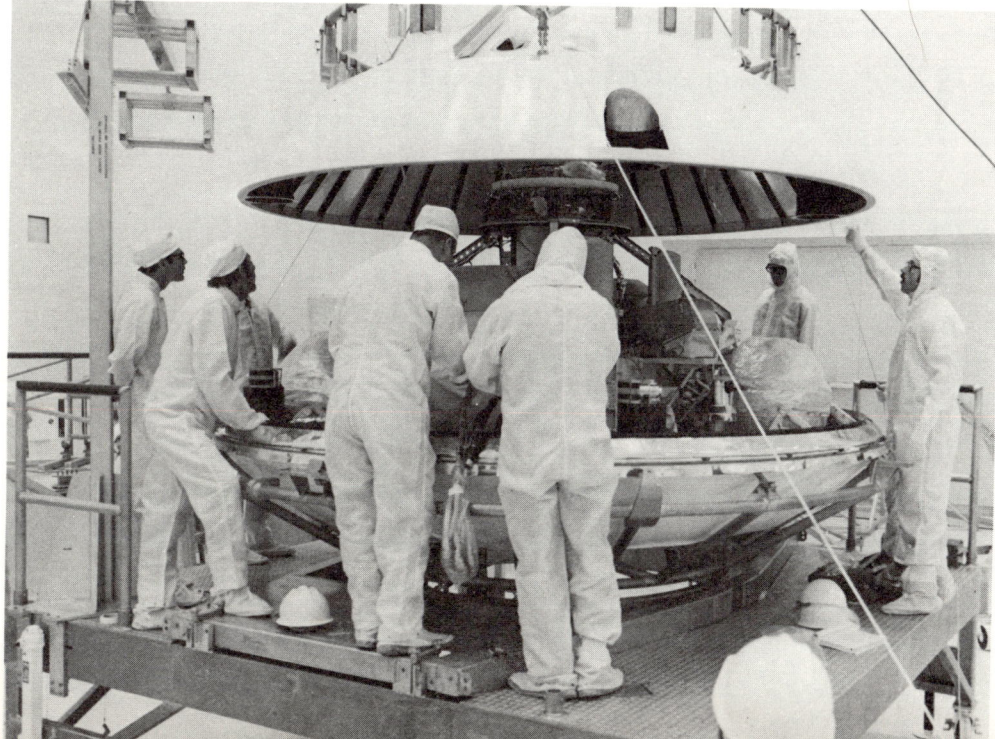

The Viking Lander Capsule is taken from its shipping crate to be prepared for launch to Mars.

Perhaps most exciting of all were the experiments that tested for signs of life on Mars. If life existed, the scientists expected to find microscopic life in the soil. Three biology and chemistry labs in the landers analyzed and tested the samples from the Mars surface for any hints of living plants or animals. Although the results are not certain, it does seem that there is no life on the red planet.

On March 3, 1972, Pioneer 10 was launched to fly by the planet Jupiter. It reached there after a journey lasting nearly two years, and radioed back amazing photos of the huge planet and several of its moons, and measurements of its temperature, radiation and magnetic field. The tiny, disc-shaped spacecraft was designed to function only long enough to reach Jupiter. But somehow it kept on sending radio signals back to earth as it sailed farther and farther away. It became the most distant object made by human beings in the universe! Then, on June 13, 1983, it passed the orbits of Pluto and Neptune, the outermost planets, and left the solar system.

Scientists now believe Pioneer 10 can continue to send radio signals for another ten years, or until it is 5 billion miles (8 billion km) from the sun. During this time scientists hope to learn whether there is a tenth planet at the edge of the solar system that they have not been able to detect. They also think that Pioneer 10 will give them more information on the boundary where the solar system ends and the interstellar space begins.

Even after the eight-watt radio is dead, the craft will cruise on—perhaps forever, since there is nothing in outer space to stop it. It is possible, though, that it will be intercepted by intelligent beings somewhere else in our galaxy. There is a plaque on board with images of a man and a woman, a diagram of the solar system and other symbols to explain the origin of the spacecraft.

In about 5 billion years Pioneer 10 should be near the outer edge of our Milky Way galaxy and entering the true emptiness of outer space. By that time, however, the sun will have swallowed up planet earth, and life as we know it will probably no longer exist. So there is a good chance that Pioneer 10 will outlive human life on earth!